JAN 3 1 2008

WITHDRAWN

WITHDRAWN

WORLD OF INSECTS

Praying Mantises

Warrenville Public
Library District
28W751 Stafford Place
Warrenville, IL 60555

by Colleen Sexton

BLASTOFF!
2
READERS

BELLWETHER MEDIA • MINNEAPOLIS, MN

Note to Librarians, Teachers, and Parents:

Blastoff! Readers are carefully developed by literacy experts and combine standards-based content with developmentally appropriate text.

Level 1 provides the most support through repetition of high-frequency words, light text, predictable sentence patterns, and strong visual support.

Level 2 offers early readers a bit more challenge through varied simple sentences, increased text load, and less repetition of high-frequency words.

Level 3 advances early-fluent readers toward fluency through increased text and concept load, less reliance on visuals, longer sentences, and more literary language.

Whichever book is right for your reader, Blastoff! Readers are the perfect books to build confidence and encourage a love of reading that will last a lifetime!

This edition first published in 2007 by Bellwether Media.

No part of this publication may be reproduced in whole or in part without written permission of the publisher. For information regarding permission, write to Bellwether Media Inc., Attention: Permissions Department, Post Office Box 1C, Minnetonka, MN 55345-9998.

Library of Congress Cataloging-in-Publication Data
Sexton, Colleen A.
  Praying mantises / by Colleen Sexton.
     p. cm. — (World of insects)
Summary: "Simple text accompanied by full-color photographs give an upclose look at praying mantises. Intended for kindergarten through third grade students"—Provided by publisher.
  Includes bibliographical references and index.
  ISBN-13: 978-1-60014-053-2 (hardcover : alk. paper)
  ISBN-10: 1-60014-053-X (hardcover : alk. paper)
  1. Praying mantis—Juvenile literature. I. Title.

  QL505.9.M35S49 2007
  595.7'25—dc22   2006034963

Text copyright © 2007 by Bellwether Media.
SCHOLASTIC, CHILDREN'S PRESS, and associated logos are trademarks and/or registered trademarks of Scholastic Inc.
Printed in the United States of America.

Scholastic   1/4/08 $20.00

Contents

The praying mantis is a
large **insect**.

It lives in fields and gardens.

The praying mantis is brown or green.

Green or brown colors help the praying mantis **blend** with its **surroundings**.

The praying mantis has a
long body.

The praying mantis has a head shaped like a triangle.

The praying mantis can turn its head. Most insects cannot do that.

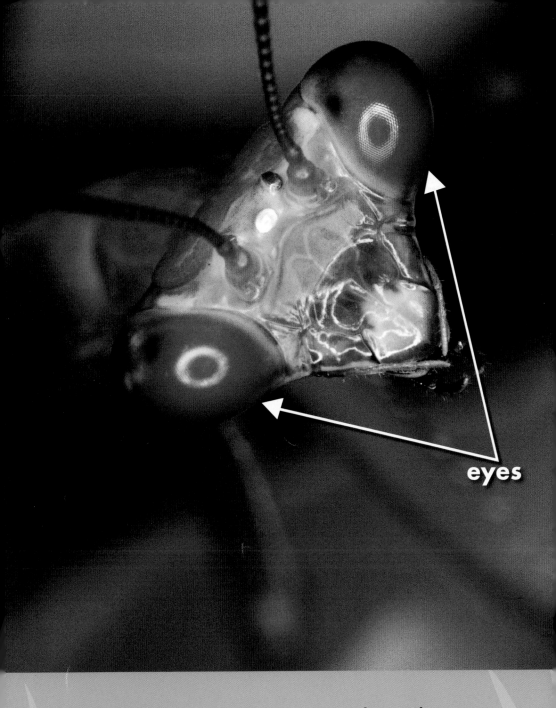

eyes

The praying mantis has big
eyes. It can see well.

antennas

The praying mantis has **antennas**. It uses antennas to feel and smell things.

The praying mantis has
four wings.

The praying mantis has
six legs.

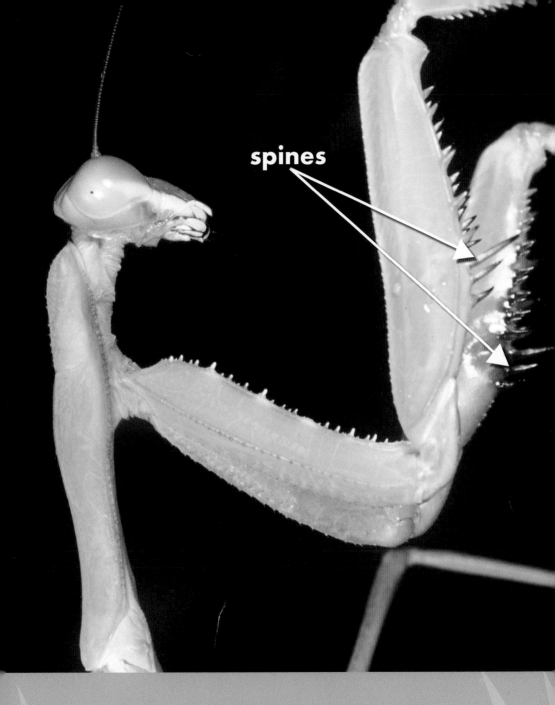

spines

The front legs are larger than the other legs. The front legs have sharp **spines**.

15

The praying mantis spreads its wings when a **predator** is near.

16

It tries to scare them away.

The praying mantis eats insects. It sits very still until an insect passes by.

The praying mantis reaches
out quickly and grabs
the insect.

The praying mantis uses its spines to hold insects while it eats them alive.

The female praying mantis might even eat the male praying mantis.

Glossary

antennas—the feelers on an insect's head; insects use their antennas to touch and smell things.

blend—when something looks so much like the things around it that it becomes difficult to see

insect—a small animal with six legs and a hard outer body that is divided into three parts; most insects also have two or four wings. There are more insects in the world than any other kind of animal.

predator—an animal that hunts and kills another animal for food

spines—stiff, sharp parts that grow on an animal or plant

surroundings—the area around something

To Learn More

AT THE LIBRARY

Fontenot, Mary Alice. *Clovis Crawfish and Michelle Mantis*. Gretna, La.: Pelican Publishing, 1989.

Freeman, Don. *Manuelo the Playing Mantis*. New York: Viking, 2004.

Hall, Margaret. *Praying Mantises*. Mankato, Minn.: Pebble Books, 2005.

Hipp, Andrew. *The Life Cycle of a Praying Mantis*. New York: PowerKids Press, 2002.

Stefoff, Rebecca. *Praying Mantis*. New York: Benchmark Books, 1997.

ON THE WEB

Learning more about praying mantises is as easy as 1, 2, 3.

1. Go to www.factsurfer.com

2. Enter "praying mantises" into search box.

3. Click the "Surf" button and you will see a list of related web sites.

With factsurfer.com, finding more information is just a click away.

Index

The photographs in this book are reproduced through the courtesy of: George Grall/Getty Images, front cover; JH Pete Carmichael/Getty Images, pp. 4-5; SIMI/Alamy, p. 6; Tim Laman/Getty Images, p. 7; Tim Oliveira, p. 8; Frank B. Yuwono, p. 9; Kim Murrell, p. 10; Gary Bell/Alamy, p. 11; Phaedra Wilkinson, p. 12; Danita Delimont/Alamy, p. 13; Frank B. Yuwono, p. 14; Paul Harcourt Davies/imagequestmarine.com, p. 15; Tim Laman/Getty Images, pp. 16-17; Lori, pp. 18-19; Hermann J. Netz/f1online/Alamy, p. 20; Jose B. Ruiz/Alamy, p. 21.